ICELAND

Life and Nature on a North Atlantic Island

Iceland
Review

ICELAND Life and Nature
on a North Atlantic Island
Project directors: Haraldur J. Hamar
and Elín Jónsdóttir
Text: Bernard Scudder
Photographs: Páll Stefánsson
except pages 22, 41, 42, 44, 51, 68, 70 Sigurgeir
Jónasson, 23, 24-25, 47 Hjálmar R. Bárdarson,
31 Gunnar Hannesson, and 72 Stefán Karlsson
Design: Gudjón Sveinbjörnsson
and Magnús V. Pálsson
Colour separations: Prentmyndastofan Ltd,
Reykjavík
Published by Iceland Review ©
Reykjavik, Iceland
First published in 1991
Printed in Singapore 1999

ISBN 9979-51-058-7

Front cover: Laugahraun lava field and
Mt. Brennisteinsalda, Landmannalaugar, S. Iceland.
Photo Páll Stefánsson, Iceland Review.

The Essence of Iceland

Capturing the character of Iceland is not an easy task when compiling a book of this size, which is supposed to reflect the Icelandic experience. A single photo, though, can speak volumes. And for that reason this book is primarily pictorial and aims to give its readers as much of Iceland as possible within this space and time.

At Iceland Review we have many thousands of photos to select from, among the best photographic material available in Iceland, and endless factual material which has had to be condensed into a tightly knit text.

Many people have contributed to its production, and we feel we have achieved our original goal of making this book both informative and a precious timeless souvenir for everyone with an interest in Iceland — those who have long-standing ties of family or friendship, as well as those who are experiencing Iceland for the first time.

Ocean for a Border

"Half our fatherland is the ocean," a well-known Icelandic poem says. For the Icelanders, in their North Atlantic island home, the sea is only in part a border, and in part a second home for this fishing nation, the bounteous provider of greater harvests than their harsh land itself can yield. Iceland was the last country in Europe to be settled, during a wave of Nordic migrations in the ninth century, and eager settlers made their home on the unpopulated island, driven on by the challenge of a new, beautiful land, a new life, freedom — and, almost instantly, the creation of a national identity, a sense of common destiny.

Like most island-dwellers, the Icelanders feel a profound attachment to the land they inhabit, to the culture and identity which, with no borders but the boundless ocean, they have preserved remarkably intact over the centuries. But by the same token, the ocean would remain Iceland's lifeline to the outside world right up until the present day. It has been the road along which all necessities and comforts have been brought that the stark land itself cannot provide, but also the channel for an insatiable curiosity towards all that lies beyond the horizons in more than just a material sense — allowing Iceland to be a modern nation in the modern world, while keeping its continuity with its own past.

And the ocean's lure has always been strong, drawing the ancient nation of seafarers on farther westwards, to Greenland and even the shores of North America, where they established settlements which were fated to disappear but whose memory would live on in testimony to human endeavour.

Icelanders live on the land, but live from the sea. Few nations can surely understand on so national a scale the moods and whims of the ocean all around them, know that its ineluctable forces can bring tragedy as well as triumph. Relentlessly pounding waves have hewn the face of the very land the Icelanders inhabit. Whole crews of fishing boats have been swept to tragic deaths in an instant; haunting sea-ice drifting down from the Arctic can block harbours and isolate communities from the outside world.

The ocean demands, deserves and is shown an awed respect. And proximity to the elements, the primal power of the seas, has fostered a belief in a providence that challenges and rewards, and an optimism about human survival on the border of the habitable world.

Defiant Outposts to the North

Rugged walls of cliffs standing guard against the sea typify much
of the northern coast which forms Iceland's border facing the Arctic.
The sheer, razor-sharp cliffs of Hornbjarg (facing) and Hælavíkur-
bjarg behind it jut out defiantly towards the north from Iceland's
West Fjords, etched by relentless waves and winds. Inhospitable,
uninhabitable and forbidding as they seem, these two cliffs are
home to the largest bird colonies in Iceland. Hornbjarg, the
northernmost point of the West Fjords, rises to 534 m above
sea level at its peak.

Preceding page: Waves lash the cliffs of Iceland's northernmost
point, the island of Grímsey straddling the Arctic Circle. A mere
120 islanders — but teeming colonies of birds — inhabit this rocky
outpost north of the mainland. Like Iceland in relation to the
continents to east and west, Grímsey is both cut off from
and linked to the mainland by the sea.

Nature's Symmetry

Solid, chunky rock at the water's edge and almost formally sculpted mountains are typical of the long and dramatic seaboard of the East Fjords.

Viewed across massive boulders in the East Fjords, the pyramid-like basalt summit of Búlandstindur is one of the highest coastal peaks in Iceland at 1,069 m. Búlandstindur stands on Berufjördur, the first of a long undulating series of fjords winding along the eastern coastline. Almost every fjord supports one or more fishing communities, and they are joined by a rough and sometimes breathtaking road snaking along the mountainsides and shore.

9

Shifting Borders

An island's borders are always shifting. Jutting out from smooth, sandy shores on either side, the lone promontory of Dyrhólaey, where the pounding seas have hollowed out a "door," was once the southernmost point of Iceland's mainland. Whittled down by erosion, it ceded that honour for a while to nearby Kötlutangi which stretched southwards with glacial deposits — then won it back. A famous landmark for seafarers skirting the south, Dyrhólaey is still known by the nickname "Portland" which it was given by British fishermen long ago.

Tranquil seas lap at the rugged rocks of Trékyllisvík (above), a bay on the almost deserted eastern "back" of the northwestern peninsula.

Might and Majesty

Iceland's landscapes are more than a wealth of contrasts; they are a living, creative paradox. Living, because geological forces are still hard at work shaping the appearance of the youngest country in Europe, thought to have been born "only" 16-20 million years ago. And a paradox because of the opposites which co-exist, their struggle for supremacy still unresolved: volcanic fires alongside glacial ice, riotous colours among sombre black and pristine white, vegetation obstinately taking root and retreating by turns. The ever-changing weather and ever-changing land do archetypal battle and make their uneasy, fragile truces as nature's process of transformation passes through endless variety in its quest for perfection.

As the most sparsely populated country in Europe, with most people concentrated in coastal areas, Iceland possesses huge tracts of unspoilt landscapes where nature's might and majesty reign supreme, clash and live in harmony. With vast panoramas of contrasting landscapes, ice and soil, lava and sand, water and steam, green grass and knurled rock, the Icelandic wilderness creates an illusion of infinite variety. And of eternity too, when the only sounds are the timeless ripple and rush of water, the singing of the wind, the intermittent calls of migrating birds.

Motion and stillness both abound, on an epic scale. Active volcanoes gushing fire and molten lava testify to the power packed within the depths of the earth, and torrents of water thunder down in search of sea level, through gorges, rifts and sheer drops where the very earth has been split by titanic forces, wearing themselves a course through tough rock and supple sands alike. Then elsewhere, glaciers, sandy wastes and stark, imposing chains of mountains dwarf human intruders and taunt them with eerie, empty silences.

Even vastness has its delicate sides. Not just in hardy plants forcing down roots in defiance of the elements, but also in lush sheltered stretches, even though this is a far cry from the country "covered with trees from mountain to shore" which ancient chronicles tell us the first settlers found. But what the elements take away, man is trying to replace elsewhere — and so even is nature itself. On the tiny volcanic island of Surtsey, formed by a submarine eruption off the south coast in 1963, pioneer seeds and spores brought in by the sea, wind and birds have already begun to take root — watched from a distance by scientists studying how vegetation colonizes the land.

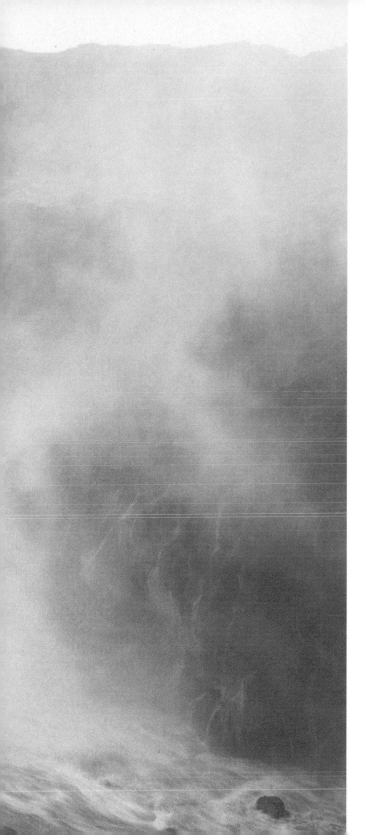

Torrential Forces

Dettifoss in northeast Iceland (facing) is the most powerful
waterfall in all Europe, with an average flow of 193 m³ per second,
despite being a "mere" 44 metres high. It is situated some two-thirds
of the way along Jökulsá á fjöllum, the second-longest river in
Iceland, which flows 206 km from Vatnajökull glacier and
northwards into the sea.

Rushing water has carved through the rock to leave a natural
bridge across the lower of the two falls of Ófærufoss (above) in
south-central Iceland.

Preceding: Skógafoss falls in south Iceland, 60 metres high and last
in a series of twenty cascades along the Skógaá river. According
to legend, a 10th-century settler of Iceland hid his treasure
in a cave behind the falls.

15

Boiled by the Earth

The geothermal forces which originally gave birth to Iceland are active as ever, giving it
the greatest concentration of hot springs and high-temperature fields in the world and
breaking up through the earth's crust in countless forms.
Strokkur in the Geysir hot spring area of south Iceland, spouts boiling water 10-15 metres
into the air every few minutes (facing). It began "performing" as activity waned in the nearby
"Great Geysir" which has given the name "geyser" to this phenomenon in many languages.
Vegetation thrives in the warmth of tiny boiling pools bubbling up at Hrafntinnusker (above),
east of the volcanic Mt. Hekla in south Iceland.

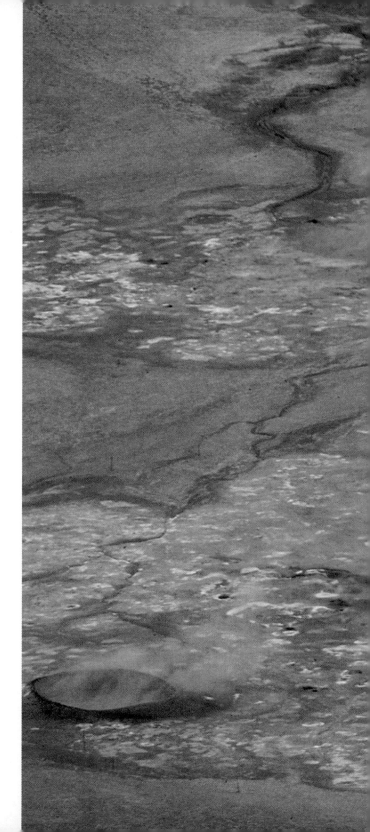

Shaped by Heat and Colour

Rich deposits of sulphur, gypsum and other minerals brought up from the depths of the earth have painted the earth at Námaskard, north Iceland. Pockmarked with steaming craters and bubbling with mudpools, it is one of the largest high-temperature fields in Iceland.

In its least treacherous area, Námaskard is crossed by a road linking north and east Iceland which forms part of the main Ring Road circling the whole country.

Intense geothermal activity at Námaskard is the result of its location on the rift which runs diagonally southwest to northeast right through Iceland and is a continuation of the North Atlantic ridge which, geologically speaking, divides the respective tectonic plates on which the continents of Europe and America lie.

Sulphur was mined in the area for export around the time of the Reformation and sporadically until the mid-19th century.

Nature's Infinite Spectrum

Shaped by the twin action of eroding ice-age glaciers and ever-present geothermal forces, the southern central highlands of Iceland are a riot of natural colour scarcely without rival.

Rhyolite formations typical of volcanic activity in some parts of Iceland, tinged with deposits from sulphurous steam, have created striking contrasts of colour near Landmannalaugar (facing). A popular spot for campers and hikers, the area is awash with variety, since bare rocks tower in places above fertile valleys where hot and cold springs blend at temperatures which make them ideal not just for lush vegetation but also for bathing.

Hrafntinnusker (above), whose name means "obsidian peak," measures 1,000 m above sea level and is often shrouded in heavy snow — but is also one of the hottest high-temperature fields in Iceland. A hot spring has cut an arch through an otherwise impenetrable cover of snow.

Outbursts of Fire and Fury

Active volcanoes are found widely along the volcanic belt traversing Iceland, producing an eruption somewhere every three years on average. Post-glacial lava flows cover some 10% of Iceland's total area, and historical flows around 1.5%.

A new volcano erupted unexpectedly in 1973 on Heimaey (facing), the only one of the Westman Islands which is inhabited. The 5,300 islanders were evacuated overnight, and lava and ash buried one-third of the town. Once the eruption was over, the inhabitants soon returned to Heimaey to rebuild and resume their way of life.

A submarine eruption (above) which began in 1963 off the Westman Islands and lasted two years added a new island to the archipelago. Named Surtsey ("Surtur's Isle") after the pagan god of fire, it grew to 3.1 km^2, but has since been eroded by waves and wind to 2.3 km^2. Already, the island has begun to be colonized by birds and lower plant forms.

Lava in Living Memory

The Krafla eruptions of the 1980s have added new layers of lava to those deposited by volcanic activity over the centuries and millennia — much of which has taken place in historical times and been well documented.

Piles of jagged new lava have built up at Krafla (facing) as an awe-inspiring monument to where the flow comes to a halt. In the eight eruptions during the 1980s, new lava covered a total area of 66 km^2.

Moss (above) is quick to cover the seemingly inhospitable new lava field with a new green cloak to replace what has been lost.

Preceding: Still a fiery red, magma flows through a channel it has cut across an earlier lava field.

Come Hell and High Water

Lakes have formed in Iceland's volcanic craters even in relatively recent times — and even shaped the country's history as much as its landscapes.

Bathers wallow in the water of the lake crater of Víti ("Hell") in the central highlands (foreground) which is still at a temperature of 22°C after an eruption there more than a century ago, in 1875. Perhaps understandably, the depth of the water in "Hell" has never been measured, but the lake itself is 150 m in diameter.

The water in Öskjuvatn (background), the deepest lake in Iceland at up to 217 m, is now too cold for bathing but also measured 22°C in 1876. A year before, the volcano erupted with such violence that ash fell 1,600 km away in Stockholm 38 hours later in large enough quantities to allow scientific samples to be gathered. This was the largest pyroclastic eruption ever recorded in Iceland, and the destruction it wrought upon farming land in east Iceland was an important contributing factor to the wave of emigration during the following decade, when one-tenth of the population left to find new homes in North America. Lake Öskjuvatn occupies 11 km² of the total 50 km² of the Askja caldera.

Creation and Destruction

Mighty volcanic fire and brimstone have been a truly living force in the popular imagination, their awesome destructive power well tuned to both pagan and Christian cosmologies.

When fire ripped open the earth at Sída in south-central Iceland in 1783, some 565 km² of lava poured out, the largest flow from a single eruption in historical times anywhere in the world. Its seemingly endless progress suddenly ground to a halt at the river Skaftá (facing), by the door of the church where a clergyman was delivering a sermon praying for deliverance, which has been known ever since as the "Fire Sermon." Soft and beautiful as the now moss-covered lava field looks today, the poisonous gases which the eruption spewed forth brought Iceland's population down to its lowest-ever 30,000 and killed off the greater part of all cattle, horses and sheep in the country.

Inoffensive as it looks on a fine day, the active volcano Mt. Hekla (above) in south Iceland was considered by continental medieval theologians to be the gateway to Hell — and not without reason, since it has erupted at least 17 times since man first witnessed its powers in 1104. And while notions of the abode of the damned have changed, Hekla keeps on regardless, with several eruptions this century.

31

Realms Where Ice Reigns

One-tenth of Iceland's surface lies beneath a glacial cloak —
but the land which is hidden, like that elsewhere, is widely alive
with fiery forces.

Valleys and rifts appear etched into the frozen orb of Öræfajökull
glacier (facing), viewed from Hvannadalshnjúkur which is the highest peak in Iceland at 2,119 m. Öræfajökull is the highest mountain
range in the country, covered from 1,000 m above sea level and
upwards by ice which forms part of the Vatnajökull cluster, the
largest glacial cap in Europe. But beneath Öræfajökull's frozen
exterior lies a mighty volcanic cone which has erupted twice since
the settlement. One eruption, in 1362, produced the largest deposit
of tuff (10 km³) recorded in historical times, after which the local
southeastern countryside was renamed *Öræfi* ("Wasteland").

Like other creations of Mother Nature, glaciers come in all shapes
and sizes. Tindfjallajökull (above) in the south seems small and
friendly in comparison with its giant kin, at a mere 26.8 km² in
area and 1,462 m at its highest point.

Glacial Mobile Sculptures

The water cycle approaches the notion of perpetual motion, but with endless transformations. One of countless glacial fingers of Eyjafjallajökull (facing) near the south coast beetles down into a lagoon which feeds a river heading for the sea. Despite its romantic sound, glacial water is characteristically milky-white or even brown, due to the load which the glacier carries with it as it moves.

Looking more like wind-hewn rock than ice, a glacier provides an abrupt border to the lush grass of Skaftafell park (above). This southeastern region regularly witnesses glacial floods of astonishing power, when accumulated meltwater bursts its frozen bounds — often taking bridges and roads with it on its downward course.

(Preceding) Icebergs calve in countless shapes from Vatnajökull, the largest glacial cap in Europe at 8,400 km^2, into the eerie and ever-growing Breidamerkurlón lagoon beside the Ring Road as it skirts between sand and ice in the southeast.

Contrasts and Co-existence

Even where there is ice, not land, under foot, contrasting contours abound.

Looking westwards from Öræfajökull, a thin glacier spreads down into the valley in front of where the Skaftafell glacier curls its way around imposing mountain peaks (facing). Myriad separate, identifiable glaciers combine to form the Vatnajökull cluster, which is estimated to be 400 m thick on average.

But opposing natural forces find ways to co-exist. Iceland's highest peak, Hvannadalshnjúkur (above), gives a backdrop of purity and almost innocence to the shrubland which flourishes in Skaftafell park.

Natural Companions

A single native land mammal inhabited Iceland before man — the Arctic fox, which moved north from mainland Europe across the retreating glaciers at the end of the Ice Age. From the north, polar bears have occasionally been carried over on ice floes but have never made their home in Iceland.

The reason for this sparse fauna is of course that Iceland was never part of the landmass which split apart to create the giant continents, but was born much later from the sea by the very forces which had long rent them asunder. So besides domestic and farm animals, man's natural companions in Iceland, with the single exception of the fox, are denizens of either the sea or the skies. Some animals have in fact reverted to the wild, among them the reindeer, imported in the eighteenth century, and the more recent mink which has escaped from fur farms.

Sea mammals also thrive along Iceland's shores, especially the harbour seal. Walruses are not uncommon vagrants in the north, and several species of whales and dolphins, some of them populous, inhabit or visit the seas off Iceland.

The true "Icelanders" of the animal kingdom are of course birds; the country is the breeding ground for a significant proportion of the world population of a number of species. This is true not only of seabirds such as puffin and gannet but also inland varieties such as the harlequin duck and pink-footed goose. Some species, such as the Icelandic gyrfalcon, are found nowhere else in the world. Geographical isolation and climatic factors mean that many more visit without nesting. A handful of North American species are common in Iceland but unknown on the European continent.

Spring and summer are the seasons when Iceland's myriad birds come into their element. Like the land springing to life after its winter slumber, the birds make their sudden, dramatic appearance, knowing by instinct that their time of fulfilment has come. Seizing the gift of the northern summer with its almost endless daylight, they nest and tend their young, filling the air with their ceaseless calls and flutterings.

With unspoilt nature always close at hand, Iceland is a paradise for birdwatchers — and undoubtedly for the birds themselves. Like their far less numerous fellow-citizens, the birds of Iceland have forged inseparable bonds with the land and the sea, and created their own thriving island home in the North Atlantic.

A Perch of One's Own

Seabirds nest in astronomical numbers on suitable cliffs, far from man-made hustle and bustle but with a characteristic noise and commotion all of their own. Iceland is home to the largest colonies in the world of several of the 23 seabird species nesting regularly in the country. Typically white with guano, cliff ledges are precariously packed with different species in numbers sometimes running into the millions, which arrive at various times of the year. Its population estimated at around two million, the common guillemot (facing) is one of six North Atlantic auk species, all of which breed in Iceland.

Between 100,000 and one million breeding pairs of kittiwake (above) are found and prefer to nest on sheer cliffs. It is one of the "patriarchs" of the gull family in Iceland, most other species of which only began to inhabit around 1920.

Preceding: "Bespectacled" and aloof, the common guillemot lives, like his human fellow-citizens in Iceland, by the sea and from the sea. Two varieties of common guillemot occur: the bridled with its trailing eyestrip, which is more common towards the south of the country, and the unbridled.

Precise and Colourful

Its somewhat affected and pompous appearance has earned the puffin the nickname "clergyman," clearly revealing the affection the Icelanders feel for this colourful and populous seabird. Between eight and ten million breeding pairs are found in Iceland, more than anywhere else in the world, especially concentrated in the Westman Islands — where the puffin is a local emblem — and on the midwest coast.

Fussy in appearance and by nature as well, the puffin prefers to nest by the sea, but on grass where it digs burrows up to two metres long to nest and lay a single egg. It returns to the same burrow when flying in from the south and southwest after winter migration, with equally typical precision — almost always between April 17 and 24.

45

Nimble Aristocrats of the Air

The uncrowned king of Iceland's skies is the gyrfalcon (facing), one of three resident birds of prey and found nowhere else in the world. Fast, acrobatic and fierce, the gyrfalcon was once prized by European noblemen but has been fully protected by law since 1913.

Gyrfalcons are not nestbuilders, but simply find rough ledges or ravens' nests on which to lay eggs, and they feed on other birds, in particular the ptarmigan, whose population they sometimes reduce by one-third during the winter. Despite this huge diet, only around 200 pairs of gyrfalcon are thought to breed in Iceland today, although the stock is not considered to be in decline.

The elegant and nimble Arctic tern (above) warms hearts all over Iceland when it arrives to dive-bomb lakes and shores and chase intruders — humans as well as other birds — from its territory. For along with the golden plover, the Arctic tern is Iceland's traditional harbinger of spring.

Some one million pairs of Arctic tern are estimated to breed in Iceland each year, arriving from winter migrations over incredible distances to southwest Africa or even halfway around the globe to Antarctica, 17,000 kilometres away.

At Home in the Wilderness

Although now regarded as a familiar Icelandic wildlife species,
reindeer (facing) are not native but were imported in 1770-78 and
released in three parts of the country. Plans to herd them were
never realized, and they soon began to breed and roam freely.
Today, they are found in the eastern area of the central highlands
and along the East Fjords, and their numbers have stabilized at
around 3,000 after sharp fluctuations, the population kept steady
by hunting. Most tend to spend the summer inland and when
snow restricts their grazing they head for lowland and coastal areas
for the winter, even appearing in villages and towns.
Iceland's only native land mammal is the Arctic fox (above, cub),
which followed retreating glaciers from Europe at the end of the
last Ice Age. Two distinct varieties are found, distinguished by
their winter colouring: the predominant blue type and the white,
and when they interbreed their offspring takes one of the two forms
with no hybrids. The fox has long been regarded with suspicion
by farmers as a predator upon sheep and lambs, but although
it is known to eat live chicks and some birds and rodents, there is
no evidence that it actually preys upon larger animals.

Seafaring Citizens at Play and Rest

Looking like sunbathing tourists, harbour seals (facing) bask virtually all around the coast, but are particularly concentrated along the south coast, which by itself is home to more than half the world harbour seal population, or some 25-28,000 of the 30-40,000 found in the entire country.

Grey seals are also found in quite large numbers, numbering around 10,000, or one-tenth of the world population of this species, and tend to concentrate on the south and west coasts.

A further four migrant seal species occur in varying numbers, tending to head for the northern coast as they move south from the Arctic. Ringed and harp seals are relatively common, the bearded and hooded less so, and walruses are also occasional visitors, heading south from Greenland's east coast ahead of the advancing pack ice during winter.

Acrobatic porpoises (above) and dolphins are a common sight off the shores of Iceland, often in large schools. Around 20 species of whales and dolphins have been recorded, and some of the smaller ones can be seen from the coast.

Living Heritage

The people of Iceland consider themselves to be Icelanders not just because of the country where they live, but also because of their heritage, the collective identity which developed soon after the settlement in the ninth and tenth centuries and has continued since as a resiliently independent branch of Nordic culture.

Above all, the Icelandic identity is embodied in the living language that has remained essentially unchanged since the nation began, and been kept free from foreign influences by a vigorous policy of neologisms. Alone among the peoples of Europe, the Icelanders today have detailed records of their very origins as a nation, in the Sagas with their dramatized historical accounts of events including the foundation of the first republic and establishment of the Althing assembly — the world's oldest surviving parliament — in 930.

Instead of ancient buildings, Iceland has the places where its history was shaped, and the precious manuscripts which record it. This is not to say that the Icelandic nation lives in the past, but rather on the past.

A distinctive culture and outlook on life have been maintained right up to the present day by transplanting foreign influences in native soil rather than resisting them, and now that earlier geographical obstacles have been overcome Iceland eagerly keeps in close contact with international trends in the countries around it, to maintain an intensely consumeristic society with one of the highest living standards in the world.

The Icelanders are now in immediate contact with the rest of the world while still being able to "keep their distance" in their northerly island home. In part due to their healthy fish-based diet, unpolluted environment and comprehensive health care system, Icelanders enjoy one of the longest lifespans in the world — around 75 years for men and 80 for women.

Psychologically, too, older people draw important motivation from continuing to work in jobs of all kinds up to and beyond the official retirement age of 67. Likewise, almost everyone gains not just material rewards but insights as well into the basic industries from summer jobs starting in their early teens. Work is regarded as both a necessity and a virtue in this nominally Lutheran society, whose small population has scarcely known unemployment in the postwar period.

A Nation's Origins Preserved

Thingvellir (facing) — Parliament Plains — is the "shrine" of the Icelandic heritage. Chosen not just for its accessibility but also, one suspects, for its stunning natural beauty, this was the site of the parliament, the Althing, which was established in AD930. Although now moved to Reykjavík, the Althing is the oldest surviving national assembly in the world today — while Thingvellir is a national park and chosen to stage the most important events in modern Icelandic history, such as the declaration of independence in 1944.

Elaborate illuminations adorn the medieval Sagas (above) in which the Icelanders meticulously recorded, in lively dramatized accounts, the events of the settlement period and their very origins as a nation.

Preceding: Testifying to their Viking heritage, "Nordic" looks are most characteristic of the Icelanders, although by no means universal.

54

History Lives On in Modern Times

There's a light air, belying very deep patriotic sentiment, to mass celebrations every year in Reykjavík (facing) and all over the country on June 17, National Day. Jón Sigurdsson, leader of the nineteenth-century nationalist awakening and movement for independence from Danish colonial rule, was born on June 17, 1811, and his anniversary was chosen for the official declaration of independence and the establishment of the modern republic in 1944.

Jón Sigurdsson's statue stands on Austurvöllur Square in the heart of Reykjavík's old city centre, overlooking the floodlit parliament house (above). The ancient Althing assembly was restored in the capital in 1847 and moved into its present premises in 1881. Construction of Reykjavík Cathedral, beside it, began in 1788 and was completed in 1796. While Reykjavík is now the modern capital of a modern nation, it too has roots stretching back to the first settlement of Iceland itself. In AD874, Ingólfur Arnarson made his home where the capital now lies, naming the site *Reykjavík* or "Smoky Bay" after steam he saw rising there from geothermal springs.

Outlets for Creative Energy

Reykjavík's old-established municipal theatre moved to an impressive new complex (facing)
in the new city centre in 1989, which serves not only for drama but also a wide range of
other cultural activities and performances. Icelandic and translated foreign plays alike
draw large audiences to both the municipal and national theatres as well as smaller stages
in the capital and elsewhere.
The visual arts developed relatively late in Iceland, with the first painters appearing around the
turn of the century, but have become one of the most flourishing branches of creative activity in
the postwar period. Today, works from these first Icelandic "masters," as well as from other
artists up until the present day, are widely on show in a number of free galleries, such as
the National Gallery (above) and Reykjavík Municipal Art Museum.
Preceding: Bessastadir (foreground), outside Reykjavík, is the official residence of the President
of Iceland. The site had become the official residence of Norwegian governors of Iceland by
the mid-14th century and continued to serve this role when Iceland passed under Danish
rule in 1380. The present building dates from 1761-66.

Healthy Life in Healthy Environment

Swimming is one of the most popular sports in Iceland, made
possible all year round in comfortable geothermally heated outdoor
pools. The largest in Reykjavík (facing) is in Laugardalur, the
outdoor, leisure and sports park in the middle of the capital.
Bracing fresh air makes the annual August Reykjavík marathon
(above) a popular event not just with the Icelanders themselves
but also increasingly in recent years with runners from overseas.
The full-length marathon skirts a good part of the capital's
coastal roads, starting and finishing downtown on Lækjargata
beside the Lake.

Moving with the Times

Although the older, healthy outdoor working life is becoming less common, healthy workouts are taking its place. Mass participation in sports and gymnastics has never been greater and stretches without inhibition to all age-groups. Women of all ages (facing) take a spin at an outdoor gymnastics display in Laugardalur, the largest sports and athletics stadium in Iceland.

Not team judo, but a modern twist to the age-old Icelandic national sport, chess (above). With youngsters for pawns, members of an athletics club give a display at a sports meet. Chess, incidentally, is mentioned as far back as the times of the Sagas, and is probably the sport in which Icelanders have achieved the strongest international reputation, with a growing number of international master and grandmaster titleholders.

Precious Resources

Fishing is more than just a way for an island nation to feed itself; in Iceland's case, it is the foundation on which, ultimately, the entire economy is built, accounting for three-quarters of export earnings.

While traditional sheep farming continues to supply the nation with food for itself and also keeps man in vital touch with the land he lives on, without the fish in the seas around it the island would be virtually uninhabitable in the modern age. All but a handful of coastal towns live almost entirely by plying the waters for this only gift which nature bestows in abundance on the Icelanders.

There is still a strong romantic and adventurous element to harvesting the bounties of the sea, but fish today is big business too. The scarcely rivalled quality of fish from Iceland's unpolluted waters is carefully maintained in state-of-the-art processing plants, and a strong marketing and transportation superstructure sees that delicious seafood is delivered in top condition to consumers the world over.

Processing and fishing technology, originally developed to support the local industry, has since become a strong export item in its own right. What man has learnt about making the most of nature's blessings has become almost as precious as the resources it nurtures and tends. Iceland's seafood industry is above all built on the pure natural environment where its fish stocks thrive. Nature has been none too generous with the mineral resources around which traditional manufacturing industries can develop, but instead has compacted pure and living energy in abundance into the very land. The might of waterfalls has been transformed into electrical power, and geothermal energy can be used for both electrical generation and high-temperature industrial processes. Both these energy resources are supremely environment-friendly — renewable and non-polluting — and only a fraction of their potential has yet been harnessed, even though power-intensive manufacturing industries have grown to account for almost one-fifth of national exports.

The irresistible attraction of pure, unspoilt natural beauty has also made tourism into a major and growing industry. Iceland's happy balance between the comforts of modern life and the drama of nature the way nature made it, between past, present and future, gives the country a unique appeal in an increasingly uniform world.

Bounteous Ocean Harvests

The ocean is Iceland's plenty — and is harvested for a variety of seafood riches, by traditional small-time fishermen and the most sophisticated industrial fishing vessels that modern technology can offer. A powerful stern trawler (facing) from the major fisheries centre of the Westman Islands plies the waters for fish to land fresh or process and freeze on board. Especially since the introduction of stern trawlers after 1970, Iceland's fishing fleet has become a world leader in productivity; and despite its small population, Iceland ranks fifteenth in global catch volume for all fish species, and even higher for seafood alone.

While the quota system on all motor-powered vessels has sometimes been said to mark the end of the old hunter society, there are still tough characters who cannot resist the lure of the sea and the prospect of a tiny share in its wealth, and set out the traditional way to stake their claims (above). As an old Icelandic proverb says, "He who does not row, does not fish."

Preceding: Haddock, caught in volumes of 50-60,000 tons per year, is the favourite fish species in Icelandic homes. Most of the haddock catch is exported, however, along with other species including cod (the leading product), redfish, saithe, herring and shrimp.

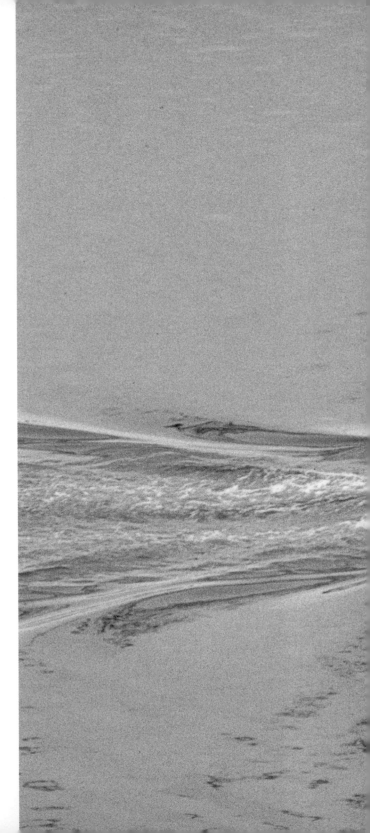

Invigorating Challenge

Small vessels (facing) still brave the ocean in large numbers,
providing livelihoods for hardy individuals and vital extra supplies
for the land-based processing industry. For demersal species,
smaller-scale boats tend to concentrate on longlining —
which is often said to produce the best fish of all.
Work on the open deck is closer to a form of craftsmanship
(above), and brings direct contact with the bracing sea environment.

Safeguarding Generous Gifts

The sea has always been a more whimsical supplier of food than the land, and its gifts need safeguarding and caring for. A mixed catch hauled aboard a stern trawler (facing) will be immediately stored on ice or directly frozen, either whole or after gutting. After landing, iced fish is either sent to plants for freezing, salting or other processing, or exported still fresh in refrigerated containers.
In today's fiercely competitive business world, it is the pure waters where the fish is caught and constant quality handling of products that have won Iceland its leading seafood reputation.
Fish farming is one answer to the fluctuations of fishing catches. Species such as salmon are mainly bred on land and grown on in offshore cages (above), although many farms rear them in shore-based tanks or release them for ocean ranching until instinct brings the salmon home for harvest. Trout and Arctic char are also farmed in Iceland and promising experiments are being conducted with breeding and rearing of saltwater species such as halibut.

Water's Power Harnessed

In the modern age, one of Iceland's greatest resources is found in the rugged character of the landscape itself which long posed obstacles to development. The abundant and non-polluting energy of waterfalls (facing) can be transformed into hydroelectricity for power-intensive industrial applications as well as general use. An estimated 55 GWh of hydropower is economically feasible to harness from Iceland's waterfalls, and only a fraction has been developed so far.

In recognition of the fact that the fishing effort cannot be stepped up indefinitely, Iceland has embarked in recent years on power-intensive industrial development which has greatly diversified the nation's economic base. Metals industries such as smelting of aluminium (above) and ferrosilicon are now second only to seafood in Iceland's export figures.

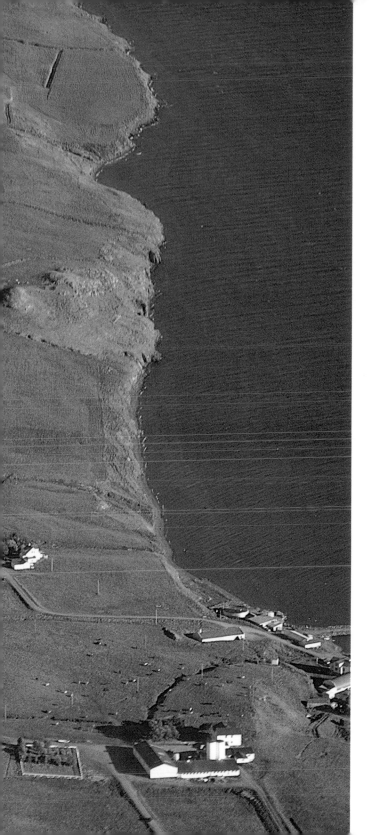

Living from the Land

Farming is as old as the settlement of Iceland itself and is the main activity for the 30,000 Icelanders who do not live in towns and villages.

While the greater part of Iceland's surface is harsh and barren, valleys are found snuggled against mountains and shores where the land is a plentiful provider. Fine pastures in fertile areas like Svalbardsströnd by Eyjafjördur (facing) have allowed agricultural processing industries to develop in rural towns and villages, supplying the entire nation with food from the cleanest environment imaginable. Besides sheep and cattle rearing, potatoes and turnips are important hardy outdoor crops, while tomatoes and other vegetables are grown in some parts of the country in geothermally heated greenhouses. Cattle rearing (above) is the second most important branch of agriculture after sheep farming, for both beef and a wide range of dairy products.

A Living and a Way of Life

Once the liveliest social event of the year for the majority of the population, the annual autumn sheep roundup (facing) is still one of the highlights of the year for Iceland's rural population. Sheep are driven off to the mountains to range freely during the summer — and highland grazing on a diet including heather and wild berries gives the meat a taste akin to game. On horseback and, increasingly in recent years, in four-wheel drives, farmers round up their carefully earmarked sheep before winter sets in and celebrate the end of the season with a mass get-together in the corral. Although holdings have been cut back under official policy in recent years, there are still some 600,000 sheep in Iceland — more than double the human population. The Iceland sheep is a distinct breed brought over by the first settlers, characterized by its lack of tail and its double coat of wool: a soft and downy layer close to the skin, with longer, coarser wool as well which is virtually waterproof.

An indispensable helper during the roundup is the farmers' faithful companion, the Iceland dog (above), which is also a distinct breed brought over shortly after Iceland was discovered.

In Pace with Changing Travel

In many ways the Iceland horse (facing) typifies the harmonious
continuity from traditional ways to the modern age. Called
"the most faithful servant" by farmers in the days before roads
were built when it offered the only means of crossing rugged
landscapes, this sturdy, hardy and reliable breed now provides one
of the most popular leisure activities among city-dwellers in the
past few decades. For many visitors to Iceland, as well, a trek through
the countryside is as much of a must as seeing the most famous
sights. There are now an estimated 70,000 horses in Iceland.
Distinguished by its five separate gaits, the Iceland horse is also
exported to "friends" around the world — members of clubs devoted
to caring for, riding and racing of this unique species which the
early settlers brought over to be their friend and fellow-worker.
Today, almost as faithful a servant to the people of Iceland is
the aircraft, which grants them swift and regular communications
with both Europe and North America and has played an important
part in overcoming the "psychological isolation" which purely
geographical factors once imposed. The hub of all Icelandic
international air traffic is at Keflavík International Airport,
where the Leifur Eiríksson terminal (above) is named after that
paragon of Icelandic travellers, the discoverer of the continent
of America in AD1000.

81

Heat and Harmony

Traditionally seen as irreconcilable rivals in most countries, industry and nature often go hand in hand in Iceland. Enormous renewable and pollution-free geothermal energy beneath the southwestern Reykjanes peninsula has been harnessed to provide hot water for space heating and steam for generating electricity. Runoff water from the Svartsengi plant has formed a pool known as the "Blue Lagoon" (facing) which has been discovered by bathers and become a popular leisure site with Icelanders and tourists alike. Named after the colour probably caused by suspended minerals, the Blue Lagoon has been found to offer relief to sufferers of psoriasis and other skin complaints, although scientists have yet to establish exactly why.

Dominating the Reykjavík skyline, a space-age revolving restaurant (above) — aptly called "The Pearl" — has been built on top of the geothermal distribution tanks which provide hot water and central heating for the capital's 100,000 inhabitants. Pollution-free geothermal heat and its natural "sister," hydropower, meet the greater part of Iceland's energy needs and keep already clean air fresher than ever by minimizing dependence on "dirty" fossil fuels.

Places Called Home

Iceland's population of around one-quarter of a million is spread among Greater Reykjavík (the capital and its neighbouring communities), mainly coastal towns and villages, and farms. Each has its different rhythm and quality of life; each weaves its own patterns into the economic, social and cultural fabric that is Iceland today, creating the common tapestry of national identity.

The twentieth century has been Iceland's industrial revolution, with large numbers of the population moving first from the countryside to the towns, then on to the Greater Reykjavík area.

In 1901, one Icelander in four lived in a town or village. By 1960, urban centres accounted for over 80% of the population, and today the rural population has dropped below 10%. Nonetheless, today's urban Icelanders are well aware of their history and origins, and most cherish regional ties of family and sentiment.

While the age-old battle with the elements is still waged on farms scattered almost everywhere that the land offers a livelihood, more people now live in the towns and communities with their strong community spirit and local pride.

All but a handful of the coastal towns live by plying the waters for the only gift which nature bestows in abundance on the Icelanders: fish. There, life revolves around the harbour, where the fleet arrives laden with the fish which gives such communities a livelihood and purpose. Some villages have little else than fishing and fish processing to offer their several hundred inhabitants; in larger townships, there are manufacturing industries as well, and services for the fishing industry and surrounding farming districts.

The "city" in Iceland means one thing — Reykjavík, home of the first settler of Iceland and now capital of the nation and home to 100,000 people, over one-third of its population. Reykjavík, the centre of government, trade and almost everything else in Iceland, has grown twentyfold so far this century and with its tasteful combination of new and old, its varied cultural activity and nightlife, presents the national profile towards the modern age. It is at once the flowering of an Icelandic life whose roots stretch way out to the towns, villages, farms and wilderness, and the claim of a small nation for recognition and acceptance on equal terms in a world now peopled largely by city-dwellers.

Capital with Natural Charm

Undeniably modern but radiating natural purity, Reykjavík lives up
to its role as the capital of a nation which lives in peace and
harmony with the world of nature. The city has grown at an
astonishing pace: two hundred years ago it was a village of only
about 300 people, around the site of the harbour, and the population
was still only 5,000 at the beginning of this century.

Today, it is home to 100,000 people, and has spread inland,
outwards, upwards, without ever losing its green open spaces and
"natural" feel. Perhaps the best proof that the city is at harmony
rather than at odds with nature is its immaculately clean air.

The glacier dominating the northwestern skyline — the mystical
volcanic peak of Snæfellsjökull, immortalized in Jules Verne's *Journey
to the Centre of the Earth* — appears almost close enough to
touch, although it is 100 km away.

Possibly Reykjavík's greatest contribution to peace and harmony in
the world was hosting the 1986 summit between US President
Reagan and Soviet President Gorbachev in the reputedly haunted
Höfdi House (above, photographed in the June midnight sun).
Preceding: Gaily coloured roofs lend toytown charm to the old
city centre, with the unmistakable spire of Hallgrímskirkja
church in the foreground.

86

Living Where Sea Meets Land

Ideal natural conditions for habitation are combined with majestic natural masterpieces all around at Höfn in Hornafjördur (facing), in the southeast. The town (pop. 1,600) enjoys one of the best harbours in Iceland — once it has been reached through the narrow straits of the delta and sandbanks which shelter the community. Dominated by the 454m peak of Vestrahorn (background), one of the few gabbro mountain formations in the country, Höfn was first settled only in 1897 but has since developed into an important fishing port and regional service centre.

With a population of 14,000, Akureyri (above) is the fourth largest town in Iceland and the uncrowned "regional capital" of the north. Living mainly from fisheries, processing of local agricultural produce and services for the surrounding districts, Akureyri is blessed with some of the finest summer weather in Iceland, nestling in shelter between the bottom of the long Eyjafjördur fjord and ranges of steep, rugged mountains.

Rooted in History

Among striking mountains in the southeast lies Djúpivogur,
an old-established community which has been a trading centre
since the days of the Hanseatic merchants in the 16th century,
thanks to its excellent natural harbour. Formerly a centre for shark
fishing and whaling, Djúpivogur is now a peaceful fishing village
with a population of 400.

Dwarfed by Mountains

Despite seemingly insurmountable natural boundaries of sheer mountains, man has settled and thrived in Flateyri (facing, on spit extending into Önundarfjördur fjord) since the first trading post was established there in 1792. Some 550 people now live in this rugged outpost where the West Fjords spread out towards the open Atlantic Ocean, living from fishing and fish processing, meat processing and local services.

The West Fjords offer some of Iceland's best skiing. Snow often remains on the pistes until Easter and beyond, and many children are whizzing around on skis almost as soon as they can walk.

A tumble (above) in the soft snow is no reason for distress.

When Winter Descends

Winter snows lend charm to man's habitations — but draw out the full, chilling might and drama of the surroundings he has chosen. Svarfardardalur in north Iceland (facing) is a prime farming district in the summer, but a trap for heavy snows in winter. The mountains towering over the valley reach 1,000 m above sea level and change between forming a natural shelter and an awe-inspiring obstacle as the seasons progress.

Horse-riding (above) is a popular winter pastime. The Iceland horse grows its own shaggy "overcoat" in winter to keep out the chilly winds, but horse owners must wrap up warm to take their animals for a refreshing canter through the snow.

95

The Year Bids Farewell

Mid-afternoon sunset sheds a strange luminosity as the city lights
come on across a quiet part of Reykjavík, the capital's patchwork
blanket of snow contrasting sharply with the heavy sheets
draped at the foot of Mount Esja.